LAUGHING STOCK

A COW'S GUIDE TO LIFE

TEXAS BIX BENDER

GIBBS SMITH
TO ENRICH AND INSPIRE HUMANKIND
Salt Lake City | Charleston | Santa Fe | Santa Barbara

For Elsie, Bossie, Elmer, and all the contented cows everywhere.

Revised Edition
13 12 11 10   20 19 18 17 16 15 14 13 12 11 10 9 8 7 6 5 4 3 2

Text © 1994 Texas Bix Bender
Animation by Dave Holl, © 1994 Gibbs Smith, Publisher

Published by
Gibbs Smith
P.O. Box 667
Layton, Utah 84041

1.800.835.4993 orders
www.gibbs-smith.com

Design by Black Eye Design
Printed and bound in the U.S.A.
Gibbs Smith books are printed on either recycled, 100 percent post-
consumer waste, FSC-certified papers or on paper produced from a
100 percent certified sustainable forest-controlled wood source.

The Library of Congress has cataloged the earlier edition as follows:

Bender, Texas Bix, 1949-
   Laughing stock: a cow's guide to life / Texas Bix Bender.
      p. cm.
ISBN 13: 978-0-87905-630-8 (first edition)
ISBN 10: 0-87905-630-4 (first edition)
   1. Cows—Humor. 2. Conduct of life—Humor. I. Title.
   PN6231.C24B46   1994
818'.5402—dc20

                                              93-48165

ISBN 13: 978-1-4236-0704-5
ISBN 10: 1-4236-0704-X

THEY MADE TOMORROW SO YOU WOULDN'T HAVE TO EAT EVERYTHING TODAY.

WORRYING

is like standing in a mud hole;

★ ★ ★

it gives you something to do,
but it doesn't get you anywhere.

Sometimes the
only way to
grab a bull by
the horns is
to slap on the
hobbles.

GOOD GRAZING makes those who are there happy, and attracts those who are far off.

IF YOU WAIT BY THE GATE, IT WILL OPEN.

The sun does not rise
TO HEAR THE ROOSTER CROW.

THERE ARE
MORE HORSES'
PATOOTS THAN
HORSES.

Moo low, moo slow, and don't moo too much.

—Duke Longhorn

★ ★ ★

"Weighs a ton, eyes of dun,
Could she, could she, could she moo,
Has anybody seen my cow?"

★ ★ ★

LET US HONOR

if we can the vertical cow,

Though we value none

but the slaughtered one.

— W.H. Aberdeen

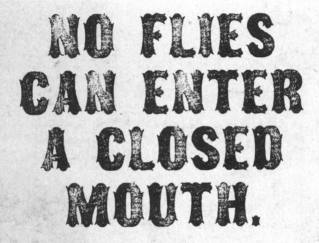

NO FLIES
CAN ENTER
A CLOSED
MOUTH.

SOME SHOO FLIES, OTHERS LET THEM GO BAREFOOT.

Good fences

make

BULLS

good

neighbors.

When you have
a cud to chew,
how can you
know about
death?

DON'T HAVE A COW

unless you are a cow.

EVEN THE POOREST COW HAS A LEATHER COAT.

THE EASIEST RELATIONSHIP
is to be a part of the herd.

★ ★ ★

The hardest is to be apart from it.

ALL COWS
LOOK ALIKE,
BUT THEIR
FACES ARE
DIFFERENT SO
YOU CAN TELL
THEM APART.

Overweight cows should rest against
objects in a standing position;
THIS WILL MAKE THEM LEAN.

With
time and
PATIENCE,
all the
apples can
be eaten.

FEAST AND YOU
ALWAYS HAVE
COMPANY.

★ ★ ★

FAST AND YOU
FAST ALONE.

It's better to be
in the back of
the herd and
be discovered,
than to be in
front and be
found out.

A RIVER
can't be measured with a taste.

Keep your face to the sun

and the shadows will fall

BEHIND YOU.

The nice
thing about
eating
GRASS
is that
there are no
bones in it.

When
you find
yourself in
over your
head, don't
open your
mouth.

★ ★ ★

SWIM!

LET THE COW
INTO PARADISE
AND LEAVE
THE BULL
BEHIND.

The only way
between a
rock and a
hard place is
through it.

TO A COW, EVERY DAY IS JUST AN UDDER DAY.

When
things go
wrong,
★ ★ ★
don't go
with them.

If you're approaching Land's End,
you need a cattle-log.

A LITTLE MUSIC IN THE BARN PUTS A COW IN THE MOOOOOD.

It's easy to be
content with
your lot if it's
a feed lot.

THE DIET
IS A LITTLE
MONOTONOUS,
BUT THE
ATMOSPHERE
IS TERRIFIC.

If you never climb a hill,
you will never know
it is different from a plain.

★ ★ ★

To err is
HUMAN;
★ ★ ★
therefore,
cows can do
no wrong.

WHAT'S A METAPHOR?

A place for cows to graze in.

One man's
sacred cow
is another's
Big Mac.

Cows have

THEIR

FAULTS,

but eating

meat isn't

one of them.

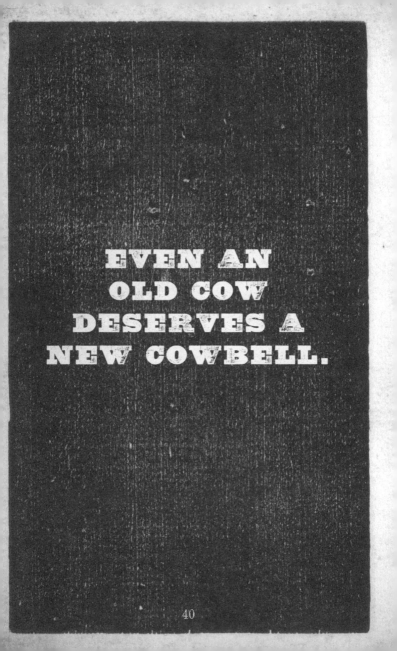

EVEN AN
OLD COW
DESERVES A
NEW COWBELL.

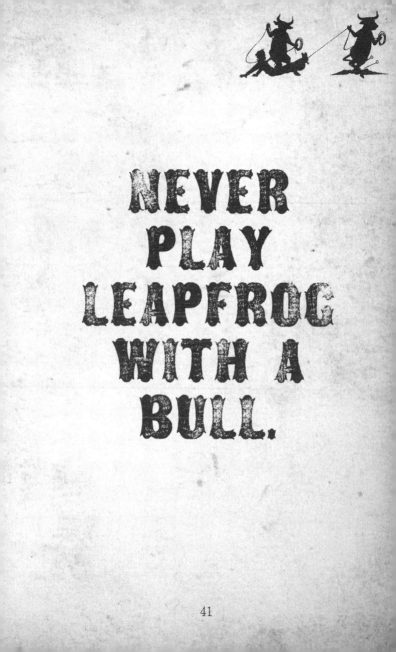

NEVER PLAY LEAPFROG WITH A BULL.

YOU CAN FORCE A HERD

to follow a path of action, but you can't

force them to **UNDERSTAND IT.**

You can always
tell a bull, but
you can't tell
him much.

Change the environment; don't try to change the cow.

—Buckminster Bull

THERE IS
NOTHING LIKE
LYING ON YOUR
BELLY IN SOFT,
COOL MUD.

You can
lead a
cow to
fodder, but
you can't
make her
THINK.

There are hundreds of uses for cowhide,

★ ★ ★

but the most important is to

HOLD THE COW TOGETHER.

IT'S BETTER
TO CROSS THE
MUDDY GROUND
TO THE HAY
THAN TO
STAND AND
LONG TO BE
THERE.

Getting off the
bull is harder
than getting on.

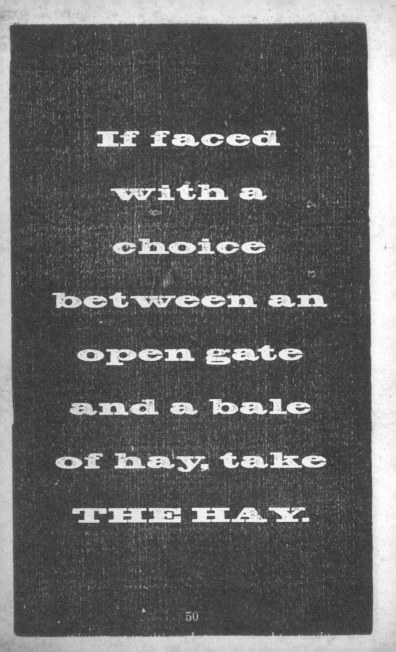

If faced
with a
choice
between an
open gate
and a bale
of hay, take
THE HAY.

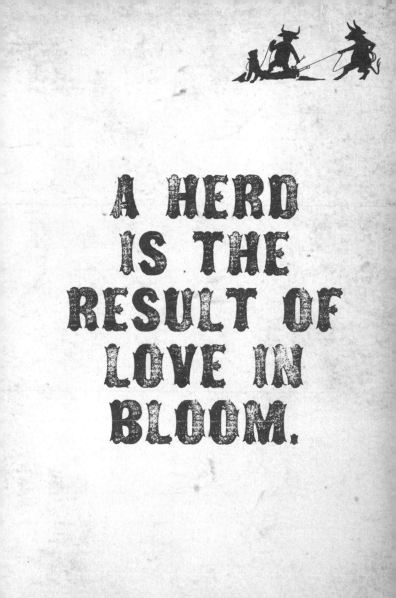

A HERD IS THE RESULT OF LOVE IN BLOOM.

I once went all day without food

and all night without sleep to enable

me to think. It was a waste of time.

COWS CAN'T THINK.

—Tao of Moo

**MOOING IS
EASY WHEN
YOU DON'T
KNOW HOW.**

TWO

HEADS

are not

better than

one, but

TWO

STOMACHS

are.

GIHO—
Grass in,
hamburger out.

When the herd turns on you

and you're forced to run for it,

try to look like you're

LEADING THE CHARGE.

Life is like a cow pasture.

★ ★ ★

It's very hard to get through it
without stepping in some muck.

If you can keep your head while all
about you are losing theirs,

★ ★ ★

you obviously don't

UNDERSTAND THE SITUATION.

IT'S NOT TRUE THAT LIFE

is just one darn thing after another.

It's the same darn thing over and over.

The bridges you
cross before you
come to them
are usually
over rivers that
aren't there.

WEIGHT AND BRANDS

ARE HARD TO HIDE.

WHEN YOU
HAVE TO
HOBBLE A COW,
A LITTLE GRAIN
SOFTENS THE
MISERY.

On a clear
day you can
moo forever.

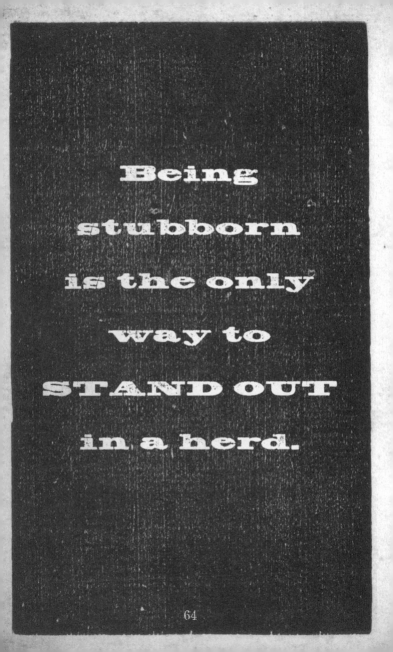

Being stubborn is the only way to STAND OUT in a herd.

There's nothing
like a stable
environment
to make a cow
contented.

A CHANGE OF PASTURE CAN LEAD TO A FATTER CALF.

If you can't be the bell cow,

FALL IN BEHIND;

★ ★ ★

you'll still get there.

When you get up to look, you lose your place.

We think as a herd.

We succumb to madness as a herd.

We come to our senses

AS INDIVIDUALS.

THE WORLD
DOESN'T MIND
A CLEVER COW,
AS LONG AS
THE COW IS
THE ONLY ONE
WHO KNOWS.

Bulls seldom
make passes
at heifers
with gases.

There
are many
contented
cows,

but who has
heard of a
contented
rancher?

TO KNOW THE TOTAL OF THE HERD, COUNT THE HOOVES AND DIVIDE BY FOUR.

WHAT IS TIME TO A COW?

It's important to understand time. The only instrument that tells time accurately is the stomach. When we get hungry, it's time to eat. Beyond that, time makes little difference.

If anyone asks
what a herd is,
the answer,
for all practical purposes,
is whatever the herd
THINKS IT IS.

If you can't see the bottom,
DON'T GO IN.

Not even a cow wants to stay barefoot and pregnant.

A good
bowel is
worth more
than any
amount of
BRAINS.

COLD
HANDS,
WARM
MILK,
AGITATED
COW.

Before the flowers of friendship fade, eat them.

—Gertrude Holstein

A contented

BELLY

makes for

a happy

heart.

**LOVE NEEDS
CONSTANT
NOURISHMENT.**

Get all the

fools on

your side

★ ★ ★

and you can

lead the

herd.

WHEN SHADE IS SPARSE, IT MUST BE SHARED.

★ ★ ★

Where have all the flowers gone?
Cows ate them every one.
When will they ever learn?
When will they ever learn?

★ ★ ★

The thousand-mile trail drive ends with the last step.

DON'T EAT ANYTHING THAT HAS A FACE ON IT.

I AM MYSELF

and all that is around me,

but if I do not eat it,

it shall not be me.

—The Tao of Moo

If you're being chased by a bull

while you're milking the cow,

go ahead and milk the cow;

you can always

SHOOT THE BULL.

There may come a day
when the cow and the lion
WILL LIE DOWN TOGETHER—
★ ★ ★
but the cow won't get much sleep.

Every tail has an end.

Two's company, three's a HERD.

**KNOW YOUR
LIMITS OR
YOU'LL FIND
YOURSELF
ALL HOBBLED
UP WITH
EVERYWHERE
TO GO.**

If you have
to run for it,
do so before
you have to.

It's better to remove a bull's horns all at once than an inch at a time.

IF YOU WAIT
'TIL THE COWS
COME HOME,
THE HILLS ARE
ALIVE WITH
THE SOUND OF
MOOOSIC.

If you're following a cow,
you should know that in all likelihood,
IT TOO IS FOLLOWING A COW.

A COW
CHIP IS A
PICNIC TO
A FLY.

A herd of a
thousand
cows begins
with a
SINGLE
BULL.

If you can't fight them,
and they won't let you join them,

★ ★ ★

find another pasture.

If you have to
climb the hill,
waiting won't
shrink it.

Swatting flies is a thankless job, but nonetheless important.

Those who know don't talk.
Those who talk don't know.

★ ★ ★

Those who moo do.

NEVER DO
ANYTHING
YOU CAN'T
MOO
ABOUT
AFTER
DINNER.

When the soul
lies down in
fresh, sweet
grass, the world
is too full to
talk about.

JUST BEING has not been
given its due. Stop thinking so much;
chew your cud a while.

NOTHING IS
SO ORDINARY
AS WANTING
TO BE
REMARKABLE.

You can cover it with sugar and bake it in the oven, but a cowpie is still MANURE.

Anyone
concerned
about their
dignity should
make a point
never to ride
a bull.

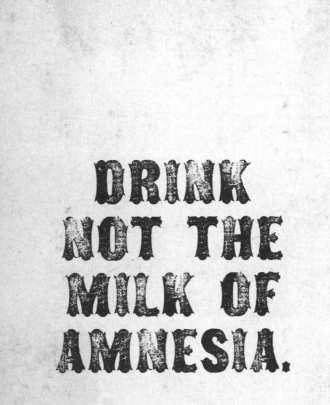

DRINK
NOT THE
MILK OF
AMNESIA.

IF YOU STRADDLE THE FENCE,

you'll never have your
feet on the ground.

"There's something in the way she moos."

THE PATH CONTINUOUSLY FOLLOWED BECOMES A HABIT.

It ain't over
till the
fat cow sings.